Edited by
Lori Jacobs Frischknecht

Book Design by
Melissa Jepsen Johns

Published by
The Living Scriptures, Inc.
P.O. Box 3952
Ogden, UT 84409

ISBN # 1-56473-156-1

First Printing, 1992

Printed in the United States of America

THE CONVERSION OF ALMA THE YOUNGER

LAURIE BONNELL STEPHENS

THE LIVING SCRIPTURES
Ogden, Utah

In the land of Zarahemla, a long time ago, there lived a king named Mosiah. Mosiah was a good king, and he ruled over the Nephites in righteousness. **(Mosiah 2:30-31)**

Many of the Nephites were also righteous, and they faithfully followed Alma who was the high priest over the church.

King Mosiah and Alma were good friends. They loved Heavenly Father and tried to obey all of His commandments. **(Mosiah 25:19; Mosiah 26:8)**

4

One day Alma visited
King Mosiah. Alma
was worried, because
some of the Nephites
had left the church.

(Mosiah 26:1-12)

His son, Alma the younger, and the four sons of King Mosiah, Aaron, Ammon, Omner and Himni, had left the church, too. They refused to believe in Jesus Christ and were preaching lies to all of the Nephites. **(Mosiah 27:8-10)**

Alma the younger and the sons of Mosiah were leading many people away from the truth. Some members of the church were committing terrible sins.

(Mosiah 27:8-10)

Alma wanted King Mosiah to judge the people, but King Mosiah would not. Mosiah said that Alma should judge the people, because he was the high priest of the church. **(Mosiah 26:10-12)**

Alma did not know what to do. He had never seen such wickedness in the church. Alma prayed to the Lord and asked for His help. **(Mosiah 26:9-14)**

The Lord spoke to Alma. He told Alma to
judge the people and to tell them to repent.

The Lord commanded Alma to forgive all
of the people who repented of their sins and
to remove the names of everyone who refused
to repent from the records of the church.
(Mosiah 26:14-32)

Alma obeyed the Lord. He judged the unrighteous people and told them to repent.

But some of the people would not repent. They enjoyed being wicked and liked to persecute the members of the church. **(Mosiah 26:33-39; Mosiah 27:1)**

Alma the younger and the sons of Mosiah would not repent either. They did not believe in Jesus Christ.

Alma and King Mosiah were worried. They did not like their sons to cause problems for the members of the church. They wished their sons believed in the gospel.

(see Mosiah 27:8; 14)

Once again, Alma prayed to the Lord. He asked the Lord to help convert Alma the younger and his friends to the gospel. But Alma the younger and the sons of Mosiah did not repent.

Soon, members of the church began to complain. They were tired of being persecuted by Alma the younger and the other unbelievers. **(see Mosiah 27:1; 14)**

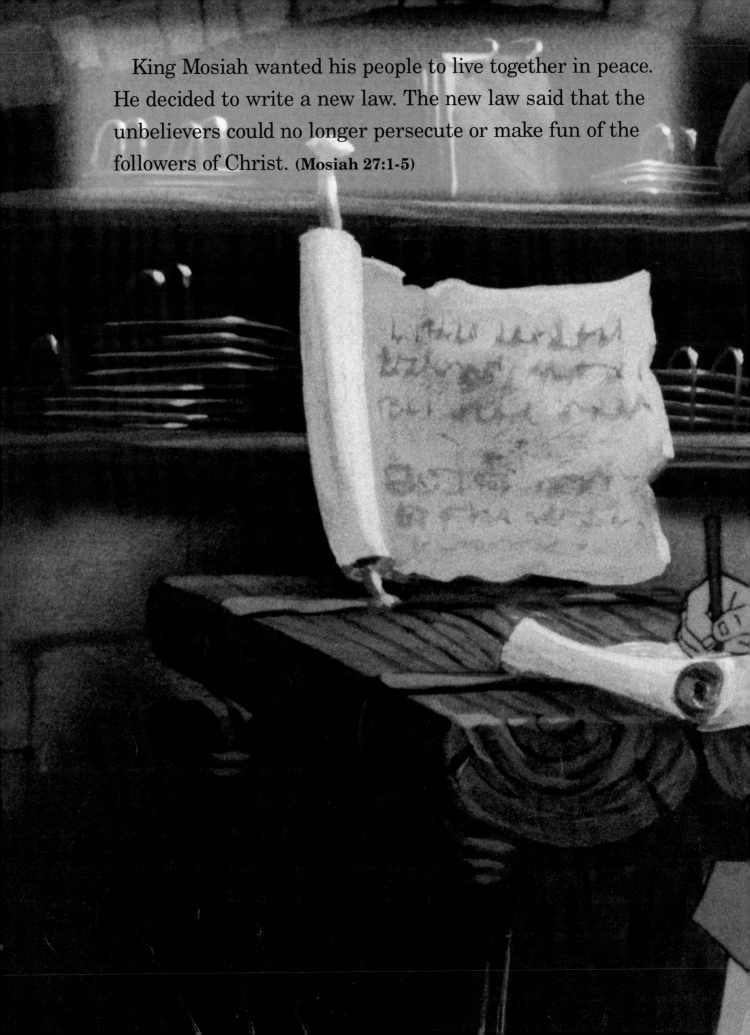

King Mosiah wanted his people to live together in peace. He decided to write a new law. The new law said that the unbelievers could no longer persecute or make fun of the followers of Christ. **(Mosiah 27:1-5)**

Alma the younger and Aaron, Ammon, Omner and Himni did not like the new law. They did not want to stop persecuting the believers.

Alma the younger and the sons of Mosiah began to cause problems for the members of the church secretly. They tried to lead many people away from the church.

(Mosiah 27:8-10)

22

One day, as Alma the younger and the sons of Mosiah were going about preaching lies to the people, an angel of the Lord appeared.

The angel had a voice of thunder that shook the earth, when he spoke to them. The earth shook so hard, that Alma the younger and the sons of Mosiah fell to the ground. **(Mosiah 27:11-12)**

The angel was angry at Alma the younger and the sons of Mosiah for telling lies to the people. He said that the Lord had heard the prayers of Alma and the people. The Lord had sent the angel to show Alma the younger the great power and authority of God. **(Mosiah 27:13-14)**

Alma the younger and the sons of Mosiah were frightened. Now they knew that the Lord was real, and they did not dare speak.

(Mosiah 27:11-18)

27

The angel commanded
Alma the younger and the
sons of Mosiah to quit
persecuting the members
of the church. (Mosiah 27:16)

When the angel finally left, Alma the younger fell to the ground once more. He was so weak, that he could not move or speak. **(Mosiah 27:17-19)**

The sons of Mosiah were worried about Alma the younger. When he did not move, they carried him to his father, Alma. **(Mosiah 27:19)**

When Alma saw Alma the younger and heard what had happened, he was glad. He knew that the Lord was helping to convert his son to the gospel. **(Mosiah 27:20)**

Alma told the members of the church what had happened to his son and asked them to fast and pray for him. (Mosiah 27:22)

The believers fasted and prayed for Alma the younger. They asked the Lord to help him believe in the gospel. They prayed that Alma the younger would receive his strength.

After two days and nights, their prayers were answered. Alma the younger received his strength and spoke to the people. He told the people what had happened to him. (Mosiah 27:22-31)

Alma the younger knew that he had committed terrible sins and led many people away from the church. He was very unhappy because of his many sins. **(Mosiah 27:31)**

The Lord blessed Alma
the younger and helped
him to recognize his sins,
so he could repent of them.

(Mosiah 27:23-31)

37

38

Alma the younger repented. He asked the Lord to forgive him for all of his terrible sins.

Alma the younger was finally converted to the church. He wanted to preach the gospel to everyone. He wanted to help undo all of the terrible things that he had done. **(Mosiah 27:23-32)**

When Aaron, Ammon, Omner and Himni heard what Alma the younger said, they also repented of their sins. They were converted to the church and wanted to preach the gospel like Alma the younger.

Alma the younger and the sons of Mosiah went throughout the land preaching the gospel and trying to repair all the wrongs they had done. **(see Mosiah 27:32-37)**

Some of the unbelievers would not listen to Alma the younger and the sons of Mosiah. They made fun of them for believing in Christ. **(Mosiah 27:32)**

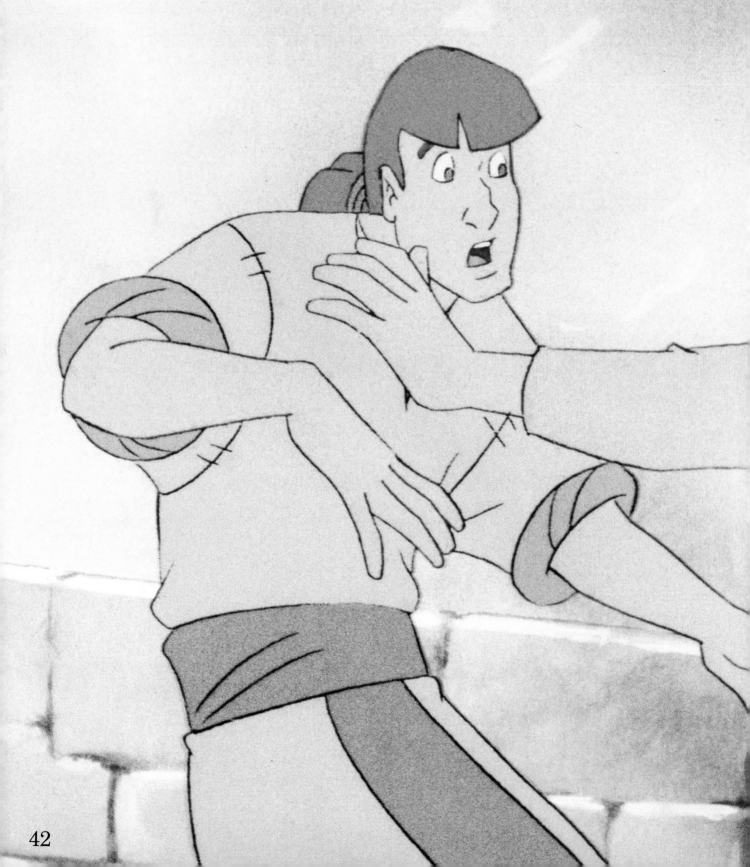

42

43

But Alma the younger and the sons of Mosiah did not give up. They continued to preach the gospel and tried to convert as many unbelievers as they could. **(Mosiah 27:32-37)**

Alma and King Mosiah were happy. They were glad their sons believed in the gospel. **(see Mosiah 27)**

King Mosiah had been commanded by the Lord to keep a record of his people on the golden plates. He had obeyed the Lord, but now he was getting old.

King Mosiah gave the golden plates to Alma the younger and asked him to continue keeping a record of the people. **(Mosiah 28:20)**

46

Alma the younger was happy. He obeyed
King Mosiah and faithfully kept a record of
the people. (see Mosiah 28:20)

"SWEET IS THE FEELING"

From the Animated Video -

THE CONVERSION OF ALMA THE YOUNGER

SWEET IS THE FEELING

Lyrics by
CAROL LYNN PEARSON

Music by
LEX DE AZEVEDO
Arr. by CINDY BONNELL BARNEY

THE FIRST ANIMATED VIDEO FROM 2 EXCITING VIDEO SERIES . . . .
PLUS COMPANION STORYBOOKS!

THE ANIMATED STORIES FROM THE OLD TESTAMENT

Abraham and Isaac is the emotion-filled story of complete obedience and unreserved sacrifice. This beautifully animated story is the first of an exciting 12 tape video series which includes these best-loved stories from the Bible:

1. Abraham & Isaac
2. Joseph in Egypt
3. Samuel
4. Elijah
5. Daniel
6. Esther
*7. Moses
*8. Elisha
*9. Ruth
*10. David
*11. Solomon
*12. Nehemiah

THE ANIMATED HERO CLASSICS

Sail along with Christopher Columbus to the new world through this thrilling animated video. **Christopher Columbus** is just the first animated story in this 12 tape series which includes such favorites as:

1. Christopher Columbus
2. William Bradford
3. General George Washington
4. Benjamin Franklin
5. Abraham Lincoln
6. Thomas Edison
*7. Florence Nightingale
*8. Pocahontas
*9. Louis Pasteur
*10. Alexander Bell
*11. Harriett Tubman
*12. Orville and Wilbur Wright

FULL COLOR COMPANION STORYBOOKS ARE ALSO AVAILABLE FOR EACH OF THESE EXCITING TITLES!

Children can follow along with their full color illustrated storybooks as they watch these inspiring videos again and again. These beautiful, hardbound storybooks will become bedtime favorites for children of all ages.

For further information, contact your Living Scriptures representative, local bookstore, or call toll-free 1-800-548-4647.

*Titles subject to change

THE ANIMATED STORIES FROM THE NEW TESTAMENT VIDEO SERIES AND COMPANION STORYBOOKS

Favorite stories from the New Testament come to life through these wonderful animated videos and companion storybooks.

Watch in awe as the greatest stories from the Bible are instilled in your children through the power of classical animation. The full color companion storybooks will become priceless treasures as they reinforce the values taught in each video story.

Your children and grandchildren will become better acquainted with the scriptures and the selfless love of the Master through these exciting productions.

Animated Stories from the New Testament include these 12 thrilling titles:

1. The King is Born
2. John the Baptist
3. The Prodigal Son
4. The Good Samaritan
5. The Miracles of Jesus
6. Saul of Tarsus
7. He is Risen
8. The Righteous Judge
9. Forgive Us Our Debts
10. The Kingdom of Heaven
11. Treasures in Heaven
12. The Ministry of Paul

For further information, contact your Living Scriptures representative, local bookstore, or call toll-free 1-800-548-4647.

THE ANIMATED STORIES FROM THE BOOK OF MORMON

Companion animated videos to enhance the value of your Book of Mormon Storybooks

These beautifully animated videos have thrilled thousands of families while teaching important, character-building ideals such as faith, obedience, honesty and many more. What better way to instill the principles of the gospel in your children.

Children will enjoy watching these outstanding videos again and again as they follow along with their illustrated storybooks.

The Animated Book of Mormon videos compliment each storybook and include the following faith-building stories from the Book of Mormon:

Nephi and the Brass Plates	The Brother of Jared	Helaman's Stripling Warriors
Journey to the Promised Land	The Joseph Smith Story	Alma and the Zoramites
Abinadi and King Noah	The Savior in America	The Tree of Life
The Conversion of Alma the Younger	Samuel and the Sign	Mormon and Moroni
Ammon, Missionary to the Lamanites		

For further information, contact your Living Scriptures representative, local bookstore, or call toll-free 1-800-548-4647.

FAVORITE SONGS FROM THE ANIMATED BOOK OF MORMON AND NEW TESTAMENT ON VIDEO AND AUDIO TAPES

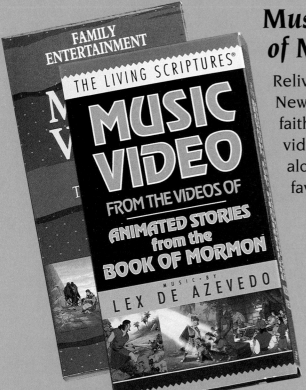

Music Videos from the Animated Book of Mormon and New Testament

Relive each animated story from the Book of Mormon and New Testament through these fantastic music videos. Each faith-building song, complete with animation from the videos in each series is included. Kids will love to sing along with the highlighted words as they watch their favorite parts from each video again and again.

Songs from the Animated Book of Mormon and New Testament on Audio Cassette Tape

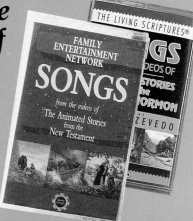

The heart-warming songs from the Animated Stories from the Book of Mormon and New Testament are available on separate audio cassette tapes. These beautiful tapes also include the full instrumental accompaniment, as well as the lyrics so families can sing along.

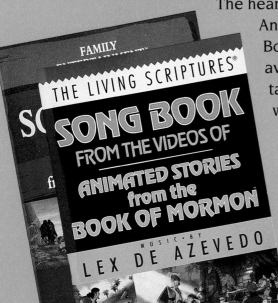

Song Books from the Animated Book of Mormon and New Testament

These beautiful musical arrangements are without equal for the best popular songs ever released on the Book of Mormon and New Testament. Each songbook also includes guitar chords for every song.

For further information, contact your Living Scriptures representative, local bookstore, or call toll-free 1-800-548-4647.